Morning Light

30 Days of Inspiration to Begin Your Day

By Bryan Hudson, Th.B., B.S., M.S.

Copyright ©2013 Bryan Hudson
ISBN 978-1-931425-11-7
Indianapolis, Indiana USA

I0162763

PUBLISHED BY
visionBooks & Media

www.VisioncomSolutions.com
www.VisionBooksMedia.com
www.BryanHudson.com

Morning Light
CONTENTS

Introduction
How to Use *Morning Light*

Psalm 63:1 *O God, you are my God; early will I seek you...*

Seeking God "early" is not only the time of day that we pray and devote ourselves to Him. Early is also a mind-set of putting Christ first in all things.

Morning Light is a collection of inspirational articles written mainly during my daily Bible reading and devotional time with the Lord. This 30 Day devotional is the first of other *Morning Light* editions as well as *Evening Light* devotionals.

I suggest reading only one per day, though it is possible to read this whole book in a single sitting. Reading one article will allow you to reflect more deeply and allow time for your other devotional activities.

Each article is followed by a brief exercise in the spirit of being "doers of the word" (James. 1:22)

Key insight I gained today:

Today's action item based on insight:

Enjoy the journey and grow in grace everyday!

~ Bryan Hudson

DAY 1 — Your Inheritance in Christ: Receive It! Share It!

Psalm 16:5 (NLT) *Lord, you alone are my inheritance, my cup of blessing. You guard all that is mine. 6 The land you have given me is a pleasant land. What a wonderful inheritance!*

We are heirs of God. We have an inheritance, even if no wealthy family member left us material things in a will. Jesus gained our provision through His life, self-sacrifice, and blood covenant. Since an inheritance can only be transferred after the death of the benefactor, Jesus died in order to transfer the provisions of His inheritance to us. ***He then rose from the dead*** to oversee the distribution of our new covenant provisions and responsibilities!

Romans 8:16, *The Spirit Himself bears witness with our spirit that we are children of God, 17 and if children, then heirs—heirs of God and joint heirs with Christ, if indeed we suffer with Him, that we may also be glorified together.*

Ephesians 1:18, *the eyes of your understanding being enlightened; that you may know what is the hope of His calling, what are the riches of the glory of His inheritance in the saints,*

God has given all believers an inheritance through Jesus Christ. We receive it through our godly family heritage, through our understanding of God's kingdom, and through our personal faith in God. We should be focused on receiving and living within the benefits and responsibilities of all that God has given us. We receive our inheritance, not only for personal benefit, but for the benefit of others and for those who follow us.

There is no good reason to live below your inheritance and privileges in Christ. Why should your inheritance go unclaimed and unrealized? You need your inheritance because it is designed to be shared and passed along. The Lord is your inheritance. He maintains your lot, or your part of the inheritance.

Key insight I gained today:

Today's action item based on insight:

DAY 2 — Vitality, Victory & Vision

1 Timothy 6:12 *Fight the good fight of faith, lay hold on eternal life, to which you were also called and have confessed the good confession in the presence of many witnesses.*

Paul exhorted Timothy, and us, to fight the good fight of faith. He gave the reason when he stated, "Lay hold on eternal life." This is not a call to salvation. It is a call to Vitality, Victory and Vision.

Vitality because the life of God is the true power behind everything we do.

Victory because our calling will be witnessed by many people.

Vision because we walk by faith, not by sight.

When I read the words "Fight the good fight of faith, lay hold on eternal life," a single word comes to my mind: *Pursue!*

There must come a time when we cease to struggle in pursuit of the things of this world and began to pursue the life and purpose of the Lord.

Romans 14:19 *Therefore let us pursue the things which make for peace and the things by which one may edify another.*

When people live in the kingdom of this world, their pursuits are driven by worldly needs and appetites. When people live in the kingdom of God their pursuits are driven by the purposes of God and the character of Christ.

Romans 14 offers a very different perspective from Old Testament days. Rather than pursuing enemies in order to destroy them, the text states that we should pursue things that make for peace. We also should be focused on building up one another.

1 Thessalonians 5:15 See that no one renders evil for evil to anyone, but always pursue what is good both for yourselves and for all.

In first Thessalonians we begin to see the contrast between the old order and the new order. In the old order people rendered evil for evil, and sought to bring retribution. In the new order we pursue peace and a good outcome for ourselves and for others. In other words, we are seeking a win-win proposition, not win-lose, lose-win, or lose-lose.

1 Peter 3:11 Let him turn away from evil and do good; Let him seek peace and pursue it.

Hebrews 12:14 Pursue peace with all people, and holiness, without which no one will see the Lord:

Key insight I gained today:

Today's action item based on insight:

DAY 3 — A New Look for a New Life

Ephesians 5:22 (NLT) *Throw off your old evil nature and your former way of life, which is rotten through and through, full of lust and deception. 23 Instead, there must be a spiritual renewal of your thoughts and attitudes. 24 You must display a new nature because you are a new person, created in God's likeness – righteous, holy, and true*

It is interesting that even though we are already born-again and new creations in Christ it is necessary to "throw off" the old behaviors.

Because we are new people, it is appropriate to change our surroundings and our mindset. This is like purchasing a house and going in to take out leftover trash, repaint the walls, and remove all items that related to the previous owner.

A new life needs a new look, a new mindset, and a fresh vision. Most importantly, we need to look like Jesus Christ, live holy, and reflect his character to everyone around us.

Key insight I gained today:

Today's action item based on insight:

DAY 4 Win the Battle for Your Mind

Romans 7:22 For I delight in the law of God according to the inward man ....25 I thank God through Jesus Christ our Lord! So then, with the mind I myself serve the law of God, but with the flesh the law of sin.

Ephesians 4:23, "Be renewed in the spirit of your mind..."

The excerpts of scripture shown above highlight the power of our thinking. While the new birth occurred in our hearts, renewal happens in our minds. The mind is often the battleground, the place where progress is either won or lost.

Below are some scriptures and suggested affirmations to help build your faith and develop/maintain a victorious mindset:

1. Mortify my mind: Romans 8:5-8,12-14

"Carnality does not control my lifestyle. My mind is the property of Jesus. Satan, keep your hands off! I am dead to sin and alive to God. I am dead to things carnal and alive to things spiritual. I am a debtor to the Holy Spirit who gave me life.

2. Clear my mind: 1 John 3:11-12

"I clear my mind of anger, envy and disappointment at others. I give place for the peace of God to flood my mind. Jesus, you are my peace. I dig up seeds of bitterness and cast them away. I have the mind of Christ." (Hebrews 12:14-15; 1 Corinthians 2:16)

3. **Renew my mind:** Ephesians 4:23

"I have the power through my Lord Jesus Christ to replace wrong thought patterns with thoughts that please God. I can root out, pluck down, throw down and destroy anything in me that is not of God. I can build and plant anything that is of God." (Jeremiah 1:10)

4. **Set my mind:** Colossians 3:1-4

"I am a decisive person by the grace of God. My mind taps into the riches of God's wisdom, knowledge and understanding. My mind is innovative, creative and productive in every purpose of God. I am disciplined in my thought life and repel every fiery dart from Satan."

5. **Focus my mind:** Romans 6:16-18

"I see clearly what I must do. There is no cloud of confusion in me. My mind will grasp everything I need to know. I cast down imaginations and opinions born of pride. My mind is the tool and servant of my Lord Jesus Christ!"

6. **Guard my mind:** Proverbs 4:10-26

"I guard my mind from the seeds of Satan. My mind is the gateway to my heart and I will protect the treasure of

God's Word in me. The cares of this world; the deceitfulness of riches; and the lusts of other things will not choke the Word in me. God's healing power dominates my body and mind. The forces of the life of God flow out of me to bless others." (Mark 4:19)

Key insight I gained today:

Today's action item based on insight:

DAY 5

When you pray, EXPECT the answer!

Acts 12:12 (NIV) *When this had dawned on him, he went to the house of Mary the mother of John, also called Mark, where many people had gathered and were praying. 13Peter knocked at the outer entrance, and a servant girl named Rhoda came to answer the door. 14When she recognized Peter's voice, she was so overjoyed she ran back without opening it and exclaimed, "Peter is at the door!" 15 "You're out of your mind," they told her. When she kept insisting that it was so, they said, "It must be his angel." 16But Peter kept on knocking, and when they opened the door and saw him, they were astonished.*

The prayer meeting at Mary's house was well attended. The people prayed fervently. They cried out to God and asked Him to deliver Peter from jail.

There was only one small problem: When the Lord delivered Peter from jail and brought him to the house where the people were praying, they did not believe that God had actually answered their prayers.

Someone even told Rhoda, "Girl, are you crazy! How can Peter be at the door and we are still praying for him?" Another "prayer warrior" told her that she only saw Peter's angel at the door. Now that's harder to believe than God breaking Peter out of jail!

The lesson is simple: When you pray, start expecting to see God's answer, while you are praying.

This text also reminds us that God is doing much more than we often realize or recognize.

Key insight I gained today:

Today's action item based on insight:

Get on your wall!
Neutralize negative factors.

DAY 6

Nehemiah 4:1-2 (NIV) When Sanballat heard that we were rebuilding the wall, he became angry and was greatly incensed. He ridiculed the Jews, and in the presence of his associates and the army of Samaria, he said, "What are those feeble Jews doing? Will they restore their wall? Will they offer sacrifices? Will they finish in a day? Can they bring the stones back to life from those heaps of rubble—burned as they are?

Your enemy doesn't care when you're not making progress. It is interesting that so long as Jerusalem lay in ruins and not fulfilling the purpose for which it was established, the enemy did not care. It was only after God gave the vision to Nehemiah to rebuild and when the people strengthened their hands for a good work, that the voices of opposition began to be heard. It is a good sign to be accused of inadequacy by forces that were more content with you doing nothing than doing something great for God.

Get on your wall today! Continue to do everything that God told you to do! Keep doing your work while the enemy complains, belittles you, and makes threats against you. It will be music to your ears as you glorify God while advancing His agenda and neutralizing negative factors one by one.

Key insight I gained today:

Today's action item based on insight:

DAY 7

Your Greater Reality: Fruitfulness and Following

Galatians 5:22 (NLT) *But when the Holy Spirit controls our lives, he will produce this kind of fruit in us: love, joy, peace, patience, kindness, goodness, faithfulness, 23 gentleness, and self-control. Here there is no conflict with the law. 24 Those who belong to Christ Jesus have nailed the passions and desires of their sinful nature to his cross and crucified them there. 25 If we are living now by the Holy Spirit, let us follow the Holy Spirit's leading in every part of our lives.*

I remember ministering to a believer many years ago who thought that if he got rid of his television, he would be able to draw closer to God. It was a false reality. While it may be useful to remove distractions from our lives, doing so will not bring us closer to God by itself. The key to living "in" God's presence (not just "closer") is not found in focusing on what we "should not" do. The key is found in focusing on our present spiritual realities.

First of all, when we were born again, both our sins AND sinful nature were nailed to the cross where Jesus gave His life for us 2000 years ago. The provision was made and it became our reality when we trusted Christ as our Savior. That's REAL, not just a concept.

Second, the Holy Spirit is at work in us everyday, helping us manifest (or reveal) the "fruit" or character of Christ as outlined in verses 22-23. Again, this is REAL, not imagined.

Third, we need to simply follow the Holy Spirit's leading. When you visit a national park like the Grand Canyon with its precarious trails, there are experienced, knowledgeable guides to lead you. All you have to do is follow instructions, keep close to your guide, and everything will be fine.

100% of my missteps come from not faithfully following God's instruction and direction. The greater reality is that 100% of my blessings come from living in the fruit of the Spirit and walking by faith in a trustworthy God!

Key insight I gained today:

Today's action item based on insight:

8 Freedom, Love, and Responsibility

Galatians 5:13 *(NLT) For you have been called to live in freedom – not freedom to satisfy your sinful nature, but freedom to serve one another in love. 14 For the whole law can be summed up in this one command: "Love your neighbor as yourself."*

With freedom comes responsibility. In this text, Paul addressed the problem of believers in Christ thinking that legalism, or doing religious works, made persons more acceptable to God. Verse Two reads, *"Listen! I, Paul, tell you this: If you are counting on circumcision to make you right with God, then Christ cannot help you."*

Of course, living right is very important. However, our means and methods for living in righteousness are not by efforts to keep external regulations in our own strength. Nor do we try to "please God" by our own standards. Our righteousness is the gift of God that was "birthed" within us when we received Christ as Lord and Savior (Romans 3:24). Now we look to God and His Word to reveal in us His character and standard for living. Now we obey God "from the heart." (Romans 6:17)

We WANT to live right because we are free from our old sinful nature. God's love saved us and gave us freedom.

Now we choose to make love the basis of our responsibility to God and others.

We use our freedom to serve one another in love.

Key insight I gained today:

Today's action item based on insight:

DAY 9 Don't Sin. If You Sin...

1 John 2:1 (NLT) My dear children, I am writing this to you so that you will not sin. But if anyone does sin, we have an advocate who pleads our case before the Father. He is Jesus Christ, the one who is truly righteous. 2 He himself is the sacrifice that atones for our sins—and not only our sins but the sins of all the world.

It is always God's will that we do not commit sin. The word "sin" is an archery term that means "miss the mark." Christians do not sin because of an unregenerate heart, but because of disobedience to God in allowing darkness to invade our light. This does not make it "less wrong" than sin committed by unsaved people.

The difference for believers is the Lord Jesus Christ. He is our advocate. An advocate is "one who pleads another's cause." An advocate is like a lawyer. When we repent of any sin, Jesus pleads our cause before God which leads to cleansing and restoration.

Repentance is no casual act. Sin is serious business because it mocks our relationship with God and produces hypocrisy by bringing darkness into light. John wrote in 1 John 1:5-7:

"This is the message we heard from Jesus and now declare to you: God is light, and there is no darkness in him at all. 6 So we are

lying if we say we have fellowship with God but go on living in spiritual darkness; we are not practicing the truth. 7 But if we are living in the light, as God is in the light, then we have fellowship with each other, and the blood of Jesus, his Son, cleanses us from all sin."

Thank God for Jesus! Stay in the light!

Key insight I gained today:

Today's action item based on insight:

10 The Dangers of Being at Ease

Jeremiah 48:11 *Moab has been at ease from his youth; He has settled on his dregs, And has not been emptied from vessel to vessel, Nor has he gone into captivity. Therefore his taste remained in him, And his scent has not changed. 12 "Therefore behold, the days are coming," says the LORD, "That I shall send him wine-workers Who will tip him over and empty his vessels and break the bottles."*

This text shows the dangers of complacency, or of being unwilling to change for the better. Moab has been "at ease" or living in comfort. On its face, being comfortable is not an evil condition, but it comes with its own dangers.

God designed us to grow and develop, not remain the same. "Dregs" are the sediment that gather at the bottom of a container of wine. Filtering wine is necessary for preserving the flavor and maintaining its purity. Wine is filtered when carefully emptied from one vessel to another, resulting in the dregs being left behind. When God allows us to be emptied out, the purpose is to leave something undesirable behind, and to enhance our "flavor" and purity.

Note some of the key words in the text that describe the condition:

"At ease" ~ Unchallenged, not growing to maturity

"Settled on his dregs" ~ An unchanged state, dwelling in things that can eventually bring ruin

"Taste has remained" ~ Old appetites and desires continue

"Scent has not changed" ~ No difference that can be detected by others

What is the solution? God sends "wine-workers" such as pastors, preachers, prophets, and teachers to "tip him over." Being tipped over is God's way of helping people change.

When we do not voluntarily practice emptying ourselves in God's presence, we get tipped over by one of God's servants who brings a word from the Lord. Sometimes circumstances do the tipping over. Also, to help us not return to our former ways, God allows the "bottles" to be broken.

Are you at ease today? Go empty yourself before Him, or be emptied by Him.

Key insight I gained today:

Today's action item based on insight:

11 DAY Yoked With Jesus

Matthew 11:28 *"Come to Me, all you who labor and are heavy laden, and I will give you rest. 29 Take My yoke upon you and learn from Me, for I am gentle and lowly in heart, and you will find rest for your souls. 30 For My yoke is easy and My burden is light."*

The yoke of Christ is an invitation to partner with Him. Yokes are used to link oxen together so that they, with less individual effort, can do the work of plowing fields.

When you take His yoke upon you and begin the work of plowing your fields of life, you will notice that this yoke, unlike any other kind of yoke, is easy. You will also notice that this burden, unlike any other burden, is light. When you ask yourself, "Why is this yoke easy and this burden light?" Look over to your side, and you will see Jesus in the same yoke with you and bearing the same burden with you!

Only when yoked with Jesus will you find rest for your soul – which is your mind, will and emotions. Nothing short of receiving Jesus as Savior and Lord, and learning of Him, will make a difference.

What is REST?

R~Repentance from sin, labors and heavy burdens. "Change Your Mind"

E~Expectation of a new life through faith in God and obedience to the Gospel

S~Salvation by grace through faith and not of yourselves. Receive the gift of God.

T~Testify of the goodness of God. Confess Jesus as your Lord and Savior.

Key insight I gained today:

Today's action item based on insight:

DAY 12 — You are God's Masterpiece!

Ephesians 2:10 (NLT) *For we are God's masterpiece. He has created us anew in Christ Jesus, so that we can do the good things he planned for us long ago.*

Did you know that you are a masterpiece? One definition of "masterpiece" is: "The most outstanding work of a creative artist or craftsman."

What is God's greatest creation? Is it the atom, the flowers, the oceans, planet Earth, the sun, or the galaxies? None of these amazing items were made in His image and likeness.

You are God's greatest creative work, because He chose to craft people in a manner that would allow us to identify with God and have relationship with Him.

The text states, "He has created us anew in Christ Jesus..." While every person is a masterpiece creation of God, those who have not received Jesus as Savior and Lord are locked out of their full potential because of an unregenerate spirit. They look like a masterpiece painting hidden in a basement, discolored and barely recognizable.

Those who have received Jesus as Lord and Savior can fully realize the benefits of redemption and new life. You look like a masterpiece painting only hours after its completion with all its vibrant color and on full display.

The best part is this: You are "unlocked" and now qualify to do all the "good things" that God destined for you before time began.

Live like God's masterpiece, do good work, and give Him all the glory!

Key insight I gained today:

Today's action item based on insight:

DAY 13 Joy in Challenging Times

Psalm 16:11 *(NIV), You have made known to me the path of life; you will fill me with joy in your presence, with eternal pleasures at your right hand.*

Challenging times will test your joy. This is especially true when you are unsure of your "path of life," or the will of God. As David plainly states, in the presence of God, we are filled with joy.

I remember many years ago feeling deeply troubled about a situation. As a result of dwelling in the "presence" of that situation emotionally and mentally, my joy began to slip away. So I took a long walk in the early evening on a summer night.

As I walked and prayed, the burden of the situation seemed to grow heavier. I remember reaching a certain point about two miles from home standing under a street light. Suddenly, an overwhelming sense of joy and hope swept over me!

In my heart and mind, as I moved away from the presence of the circumstances, and moved into the presence of God, it was only a matter of time before joy "caught up" to me under that street light.

I like to think of joy in two ways: Inward and Outward. Inward joy is what you know. Outward joy is how you respond.

Inward joy is an inward satisfaction that your are living in the will of God and are pleasing God.

Outward joy is to be glad and rejoice in the victories and triumphs that you have received.

Some Sources of Joy:

Joy comes from abiding in the presence of the Lord. Psalms 16:11

Joy comes from discovering the will of God through His Word. John 15:11; Jeremiah 15:16

Joy is part of the Kingdom of God ("Your kingdom come") Romans 14:17

Joy is a "fruit" or characteristic of the Holy Spirit within our spirit. Galatians 5:22

Victorious outcomes magnify joy!

Key insight I gained today:

Today's action item based on insight:

14 Shake Off the Dust & Stay Filled

Acts 13:49 *And the word of the Lord was being spread throughout all the region. 50 But the Jews stirred up the devout and prominent women and the chief men of the city, raised up persecution against Paul and Barnabas, and expelled them from their region. 51 But they shook off the dust from their feet against them, and came to Iconium. 52 And the disciples were filled with joy and with the Holy Spirit.*

Like Paul and Barnabas, learn to "shake off the dust" of opposition to God's plan and purpose. Let the Word spread and the disciples of Christ be filled with joy and the Holy Spirit!

There will be challenge or opposition to doing God's will, but this is actually **NO BARRIER** to doing what He has planned for you! The key is to stay filled with joy and the Holy Spirit.

Key insight I gained today:

Today's action item based on insight:

15 DAY Why Your Critics Don't "Get It"

Below is a great quote to reflect upon when dealing with critics who are not "in the arena" but only standing on the sidelines, talking and not doing. Even Jesus *"...Learned obedience by the things which He suffered."* (Hebrews 5:8)

Critics, like sports fans, have the luxury of risking nothing while finding fault with those who risk it all, everyday.

"It is not the critic who counts: not the man who points out how the strong man stumbles or where the doer on deeds could have done better. The credit belongs to the man who is actually in the arena, whose face is marred by dust and sweat and blood, who strives valiantly, who errs and comes up short again and again, because there is no effort without error or shortcoming, but who knows the great enthusiasms, the great devotions, who spends himself for a worthy cause; who, at the best, knows, in the end, the triumph of high achievement, and who, at the worst, if he fails, at least he fails while daring greatly, so that his place shall never be with those cold and timid souls who knew neither victory nor defeat." ~ Theodore Roosevelt

"Citizenship in a Republic," Speech at Sorbonne, Paris, April 23, 1910

Key insight I gained today:

Today's action item based on insight:

16 Grace For Grace

John 1:14 *And the Word became flesh and dwelt among us, and we beheld His glory, the glory as of the only begotten of the Father, full of grace and truth...16 And of His fullness we have all received, and grace for grace.*

We have received Jesus' "fullness." Fullness is: "the quality or condition of being full or complete."

Is there anything in your life that is not full or is incomplete? Jesus wants you full and complete! But not only that, He wants you to get into fullness so that you can go fill up other people. That is what it means to have "grace for grace." You've got enough grace in your space to give grace to others.

Did you go to school to only get a degree? I hope not. You went to school to get enough knowledge and skill to enable you to positively impact others.

Did you accept a call to leadership or ministry just to stand in front of people? No. You received that grace to empower you to impart the life of God to others through the Holy Spirit.

God gave you grace for grace! That's exactly what Jesus did both for sinful humanity and for His church.

Key insight I gained today:

Today's action item based on insight:

DAY 17 — Your Song of Ascent

Psalm 126:1 (NLT) A song for the ascent to Jerusalem. When the LORD restored his exiles to Jerusalem, it was like a dream! 2 We were filled with laughter, and we sang for joy. And the other nations said, "What amazing things the LORD has done for them." 3 Yes, the LORD has done amazing things for us! What joy! 4 Restore our fortunes, LORD, as streams renew the desert. 5 Those who plant in tears will harvest with shouts of joy. 6 They weep as they go to plant their seed, but they sing as they return with the harvest.

With all the challenges the people of Israel faced, there were times when they could rejoice in God's deliverance. This Psalm is called "A song for the ascent to Jerusalem." Note the word "ascent." To ascend is to go up. Returning from exile to Jerusalem felt like going UP after having experienced a season of going DOWN.

Because of Jesus, we can rejoice that we have ascended to a new life that is being renewed day by day. Today and everyday, we can rejoice, singing songs of joy, and enjoy laughter, all the while letting our light shine so others can see that we have been blessed by a mighty and loving God.

We may experience difficult seasons even while we are trusting in God. These seasons may produce tears, but our tears show our trust and devotion in God as we continue to plant seeds of faith.

Such faith and faithfulness never goes unrewarded. Harvest always follows seedtime. Our God is faithful and he keeps all his promises!

God's streams bring renewal to your desert-like places!

Key insight I gained today:

Today's action item based on insight:

18 God's Unfailing Love and Faithfulness

Psalms 117:1 (NLT) Praise the LORD, all you nations. Praise him, all you people of the earth. 2 For he loves us with unfailing love; the faithfulness of the LORD endures forever. Praise the LORD!

This verse from Psalms 117 reminds me of how little God asks of us in contrast to how much He gives us.

It is amazing that we are the recipients of God's "unfailing love" and a divine faithfulness that endures forever. If you have ever been on the receiving end of *failing love*, you know what I mean. If you have ever witnessed people make lame excuses, break their promises, or walk out of your life, you have experienced failed love and unfaithfulness. Of course, if someone's love has failed, faithfulness doesn't have a chance. Selfishness weakens human love, causing it to fail. At the same time, we must examine ourselves in this regard.

More importantly, you are also blessed to know people who love you with God's unfailing love.

These circumstances serve to remind us in Whom to place our ultimate confidence. It's okay to trust people, but that trust should never exceed our confidence in the

One whose love absolutely never fails, who never offers excuses, and who will never walk away from you.

If you are thankful to the Lord for His unfailing love and enduring faithfulness, take a little time right now and do what David said, "Praise the Lord!"

Key insight I gained today:

Today's action item based on insight:

19 Why the Seasons Sing

Isaiah 55:12 *For you shall go out with joy, And be led out with peace; The mountains and the hills shall break forth into singing before you, And all the trees of the field shall clap their hands.*

In the fall I usually take time out to do something I thoroughly enjoy, taking photographs. A photograph captures a narrow slice of time and preserves it for later reflection and sharing with others. All the beautiful trees in their fall colors will be bare in a few weeks. The same trees will glisten with snow and icicles during winter time.

Many of us dread the onset of winter because the weather deprives us of many outside activities. I remember carrying that bad attitude until I decided to take photographs after a snowfall some years ago. I realized that the snow made drab landscapes beautiful and reflected light in unusual ways.

Every season has its "song." The text states that God's creation "shall break forth into singing" right in front of us. Usually, we don't stop to notice this "singing" because the challenges of life tend to dominate all of our senses. I am not suggesting that we ignore the business or challenges at hand. I am suggesting that we make room in our hearts for the words of God through Isaiah to his generation and to ours.

If we daily "go out with joy" and "be led out with peace," we will see everything differently. Even the trees, hills and snow will seem to clap their hands in praise to God. No, this won't pay the bills, but it will be a source of encouragement and will help keep us in faith to receive God's best.

Key insight I gained today:

Today's action item based on insight:

20 Controlled By Love

2 Corinthians 5:13 *(NLT) If it seems we are crazy, it is to bring glory to God. And if we are in our right minds, it is for your benefit. 14 Either way, Christ's love controls us. Since we believe that Christ died for all, we also believe that we have all died to our old life.*

Why do we do the things we do? Is it because of fear, a religious spirit, for money, for the praise of others, or other lesser reasons? Love is the best motivator. Paul said, "Christ's love controls us."

We can only be fully controlled by love after the death of everything else. This is why Jesus died for all of us, so that all of our ungodly deeds and motivations could also be put to death.

2 Corinthians 5:15 states, *"He died for everyone so that those who receive his new life will no longer live for themselves. Instead, they will live for Christ, who died and was raised for them."*

God gives us the power to be controlled by His love, which is evidenced by not being selfishly motivated, living for Christ, and serving God's purpose.

Being controlled by love has benefits:

- Purifies our motivations
- Sanctifies our actions

* Ratifies our decisions
* Clarifies our purpose

If I seem crazy sometimes, it's just that I'm radically committed to *Loving God, Loving People and Serving the World!*

Key insight I gained today:

Today's action item based on insight:

DAY 21 Flexible Purpose and Inflexible Wineskins

Matthew 9:16 *No one sews a patch of unshrunk cloth on an old garment, for the patch will pull away from the garment, making the tear worse. 17 Neither do people pour new wine into old wineskins. If they do, the skins will burst; the wine will run out and the wineskins will be ruined. No, they pour new wine into new wineskins, and both are preserved.*

New cloth (not yet shrunken by washing) and old cloth should not be sewn together. New wine (unfermented grape juice) should not be put into old, inflexible containers.

Understanding conditions is important. Being flexible and willing to change or adapt throughout life is also important. The cloths represented conditions and the new wine/wineskins represented change and flexibility/inflexibility.

The science and logic behind what Jesus said is easy to understand. What is more difficult is to pay attention to the changing conditions and dynamics of our lives and activities. In context, Jesus talked about conditions in His day in which religious leaders, like the Pharisees, who resisted Christ and the then-emerging Kingdom of God. Like old stiff wineskin containers, their inflexibility to the expanding " new wine" of God's purpose was unacceptable.

Today, we must evaluate our conditions, and our hearts, to determine what things, if any, may prevent us from being containers of " new wine" — in whatever ways this may be applicable to our lives.

Key insight I gained today:

Today's action item based on insight:

DAY 22

Meet Opportunities With Faith, Not Fear

Matthew 8:26 *He replied, "You of little faith, why are you so afraid?" Then he got up and rebuked the winds and the waves, and it was completely calm.*

Jesus woke up to do something that His disciples should have done. Jesus was resting in the boat after a long day of ministry.

A sudden storm made the disciples afraid. They allowed their fear to interfere with their faith. Because of this, Jesus called His own disciples' faith " little." He expected much more from men who had been trained " on the job."

When storms come, or big opportunities are presented, let your faith rise, not your fears.

Key insight I gained today:

Today's action item based on insight:

Cleaning House

Nehemiah 13:11 (NLT) *I immediately confronted the leaders and demanded, " Why has the Temple of God been neglected?" Then I called all the Levites back again and restored them to their proper duties.*

An important part of the restoration and revival that God brought to Israel under the ministry of Nehemiah was a fresh focus on worshipping and serving God. During the Old Testament era, the work of the Levites, or priests, in the temple of God was essential.

Because of unfaithfulness and corruption, support for the Levites was neglected and people like Tobiah were allowed to use the Temple of God for personal gain.

When Nehemiah saw this, he immediately threw Tobiah, his " crew," and all his stuff out of the Temple! (v. 8) He brought the Levites back in and commanded the people to resume bringing tithes that provided support for the Levites and their families.

In our day, there are times when we need to " clean house" as well. Together, we are the Body of Christ and God's Temple. Our " Tobiahs" look like disobedience, selfishness, stinginess, and other behaviors that are beneath our higher calling in Jesus Christ.

Key insight I gained today:

Today's action item based on insight:

24 Ask, Thank, and Activate

Psalm 104:13 (NLT) *You send rain on the mountains from your heavenly home, and you fill the earth with the fruit of your labor. 14 You cause grass to grow for the cattle. You cause plants to grow for people to use. You allow them to produce food from the earth.*

The entirety of Psalm 104 shows God's provision and order for His creation and His people. He has set both natural and spiritual laws into motion.

Too often, we are standing still asking God to do something that He has already provided. If I need light in a house that has electricity, I don't need to ask and then stand around waiting for illumination. I need to go plug into the provision.

God is still sovereign, active and merciful, so He brings unexpected blessings. However, most of what we need is already available by asking, thanking and activating God's promises already provided in the Word of God, the Bible.

James put it this way: *" But he who looks into the perfect law of liberty and continues in it, and is not a forgetful hearer but a doer of the work, this one will be blessed in what he does." (James 1:25)*

Key insight I gained today:

Today's action item based on insight:

DAY 25

The Bright Path

Proverbs 4:18 *But the path of the just is like the shining sun, That shines ever brighter unto the perfect day. 19 The way of the wicked is like darkness; They do not know what makes them stumble.*

The "Principle of the Path"[1] states: It's not our intentions that shape our lives, it is the path that we choose to take.

Every path, or road, leads somewhere. Poor choices put us on a path leading towards darkness and heartbreak. Good choices put us on a path towards greater light and fruitful purpose.

When you are on God's path, you might even start out in a place that looks dim. Because you are committed to serving His purpose and keeping covenant with God's family, your path will grow brighter day by day.

---

[1] A term coined by Pastor Andy Stanley

Key insight I gained today:

Today's action item based on insight:

26   Overcoming Feeling Overwhelmed

Psalms 102:27 *(NLT) But you are always the same; your years never end. 28 The children of your people will live in security. Their children's children will thrive in your presence.*

This Psalm of David began with the words, *" A prayer of one overwhelmed with trouble, pouring out problems before the Lord..." (v. 1)* David reflected the pressure he was feeling back to God. David, as a shepherd, was also carrying a burden of care for the people he served. In another era, Peter said, *"Cast all your cares on him because he cares for you."* (1 Peter 5:7)

In God's presence, tell Him everything that is on your heart, including your concern for others. This is not to inform the Lord, because He knows all things. You "cast it" so that you will not continue to carry that pain, disappointment, or pressure after spending time with the Lord.

Problems don't cease to exist after you give them to the Lord, but the absence of feeling overwhelmed makes it easier for you to find answers and see solutions.

The closing words of Psalms 102:27 shows David's resolution and encouragement as he ended his time with the Lord by recognizing that God alone offers *stability, security and future success.*

Key insight I gained today:

Today's action item based on insight:

DAY 27 · Stop Wandering & Weeping: Listen to Your Teachers

Isaiah 30:20-21 *...Yet your teachers will not be moved into a corner anymore, But your eyes shall see your teachers. 21 Your ears shall hear a word behind you, saying, "This is the way, walk in it," Whenever you turn to the right hand Or whenever you turn to the left.*

I once heard a saying, "Everyone goes through a teacher." It is a true statement. While we can learn a lot on our own, we learn best from those who are trained and gifted to teach. Preaching inspires us, but teaching trains us. You can run fast after great preaching, but you'll run long after good teaching.

Isaiah spoke a word of restoration to his generation, and we speak to our generation. Isaiah 30:19 states, *"For the people shall dwell in Zion at Jerusalem; You shall weep no more."* In order to dwell successfully in any place and to avoid the weeping that comes from our own errors, we need teachers.

We need Bible teachers as well as teachers who have knowledge and skill in our areas of need. Some of the worse teachers are your friends and non-parent family members, who are more committed to making you happy than telling you the truth.

As the text indicates, teachers often end up moved into a corner because they are not saying what people want to hear. It is foolish not to listen to a teacher who has walked the path you are attempting to walk, just because you don't like how the teaching makes you feel sometimes. A good teacher isn't as concerned about your feelings as your welfare.

Take Isaiah's advice, go find and listen to your teachers. When you hear their voice, you will also hear God's voice saying, *"Here is the way, walk in it."*

When you listen, learn and do, your wandering and weeping will come to an end.

Key insight I gained today:

Today's action item based on insight:

28 Tighten Up Your Thinking

1 Peter 1:13 *Therefore gird up the loins of your mind, be sober, and rest your hope fully upon the grace that is to be brought to you at the revelation of Jesus Christ. 14 as obedient children, not conforming yourselves to the former lusts, as in your ignorance.*

Your loins is the pelvic region of your body. In ancient times "girding the loins" meant to gather up long garments and tighten them up around your hips and waist so that you could run, do battle, or do something productive without tripping.

Have you ever seen a young man trying to run with his pants sagging? Have you ever had the experience of getting some loose garment caught on something? This shows the importance of girding your loins.

To "gird up the loins of your mind" is to put your mind and thinking in a position to be useful to the Spirit of God, and not to your flesh. To be sober is to take a serious attitude. Resting upon the grace of God means to rely upon the power of God so that we can live in obedience to Him and avoid the condition of reverting back to our old ways.

The saying is true; "A mind is a terrible thing to waste."

Key insight I gained today:

Today's action item based on insight:

29 : Hope is a Choice

Colossians 1:27 *To them God willed to make known what are the riches of the glory of this mystery among the Gentiles: which is Christ in you, the hope of glory.*

J.B. Phillips translation says: *"...Christ in you, the hope of all glorious things to come."* This reveals that every hope that God has put in your heart will have a glorious manifestation. Nothing in God is mediocre or insignificant.

The key to realizing the "hope of glory" is to know that Jesus lives on the inside of us and desires to express Himself in fulfillment of every hope.

Hope is not based on circumstances, but our interpretation of the outcome of circumstances. Like the 12 spies in Numbers 13, either you interpret the "giants" are stronger than you, or you interpret that you are "well able," with God's help, to overcome giant-type obstacles.

Hope is a choice. Choose well.

Key insight I gained today:

Today's action item based on insight:

What is the Condition of Your Heart (Soil)?

DAY 30

Luke 8:11(NLT) *This is the meaning of the parable: The seed is God's word. 12 The seeds that fell on the footpath represent those who hear the message, only to have the devil come and take it away from their hearts and prevent them from believing and being saved. 13 The seeds on the rocky soil represent those who hear the message and receive it with joy. But since they don't have deep roots, they believe for a while, then they fall away when they face temptation. 14 The seeds that fell among the thorns represent those who hear the message, but all too quickly the message is crowded out by the cares and riches and pleasures of this life. And so they never grow into maturity. 15 And the seeds that fell on the good soil represent honest, good-hearted people who hear God's word, cling to it, and patiently produce a huge harvest.*

You are responsible for the condition of the "soil" of your heart and attitude. Good seed is wasted on bad soil with weeds. Good seed (the Word) thrives in good soil.

Three bad conditions to avoid:

1. "**Wayside**" is the walking path around the garden. Nothing is planted and seed is wasted. The devil "takes away" unplanted seed.

2. "**Shallow**" is a lack of depth. It's like saying "Amen!" to the Word, but doing nothing else. What was sown on Sunday is gone by Tuesday.

3. "**Distractions**" choke progress that has been made, like aggressive weeds in a garden that harm the plants. Jesus said that "cares, riches, and pleasures of life" can crowd out or choke good things.

One good condition to cultivate:

"**Receptivity**" to God's Word: Be eager to hear and act on what God said, after you say, "Amen!"

Key insight I gained today:

Today's action item based on insight:

About the Author

Rev. Bryan Hudson has a multifaceted ministry and professional expertise focused on inspiring and empowering people to know God and achieve the best in their lives. Bryan's training has enabled him to merge ministry with media: Th.B. (Theology), B.S. (Media Arts & Science), M.S. (Education: Instructional Systems Technology).

As a writer, educator, producer, and Bible teacher, Bryan communicates insights on important issues and technologies to deliver solutions to people in need as well as equip leaders to effectively serve their organizations and communities.

He is the founder and senior pastor of *New Covenant Church & Ministries* in Indianapolis, Indiana. Bryan also directs *Vision Communications*, a progressive multimedia firm that creates cutting-edge traditional media and new media. He has conducted summer multimedia training workshops for young men and women to equip and inspire them to use new media in positive ways.

As an instructional designer and adjunct professor, Bryan Hudson developed and taught a 300-level course at *Crossroads Bible Colleg*e in Indianapolis, *New Media for Urban Ministry*.

Bryan is married to Patricia Hudson, a public school educator. They have four grown children and reside in Indianapolis, Indiana.

Twitter: @ChurchMediaGuy
NewCovenant.org
VisionMultimedia.org
VisioncomSolutions.com